WALL STREET SMARTS

YUL SPENCER

IAM Enterprises

CONTENTS

Disclaimer	v
Join The Thousandaire Movement	vii
Introduction	xi
Sense of Urgency	1
Objectives	24
Greater Fools Create MOS	31
One Thousand Dollars	45
Thoughts to Live By	60
Spencer's Sources	62
Thousandaire Movement	65
Please Leave a Review!	67
More Books From Yul Spencer	69
About the Author	71
Full Disclaimer	75

DISCLAIMER

Neither IAM Enterprises, nor any of its directors, officers, shareholders, personnel, representatives, agents, or independent contractors (collectively, the "Operator Parties") are licensed financial advisers, registered investment advisers or registered broker-dealers. None of the Operator Parties are providing investment, financial, legal, or tax advice, and nothing on www.wallstsmarts.com (henceforth, "the Site") or in the Wall Street-Smart Series of books, should be construed as such by you. The books and the Site should be used as educational, informational and entertainment purposes only and are not replacement for professional investment advice.

THERE IS HIGH RISK IN TRADING!

The full disclaimer may be found at the end of this book.

JOIN THE THOUSANDAIRE MOVEMENT

Thousandaire members get unique items and are always the first to hear about Yul Spencer's new books, publications and public appearances.

See the back of the book for details on how to sign up.

This book was written in response to America's $400.00 financial crisis.

INTRODUCTION

LET ME INTRODUCE MYSELF! I'm Yul Spencer, but you can call me Spencer. As a professional stand-up comic, I've been using that introduction for most of my career in auditions, films, plays, concerts, and comedy shows. But now, with this book, I'm going mainstream.

I use this intro to relax you. You're relaxed, right? I want you to clearly understand that you're not reading material from some dude with one hundred degrees and a head full of backtests and trading history. Not a lot of technical shit here; we'll leave that up to the technicians. As a matter of fact, I see this book as a "how to" book...a "how to not stay broke" book. A way to put an end to broke-ness.

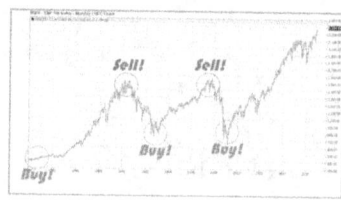

This book series' focus will be to help my fellow Americans who have less than $400 in their bank accounts to get into the "Wall Street Game." A financial crisis has begun, and I feel I have to do my part to serve. Nevertheless, the focus will be on the new investor and the trader who just got started in the markets this week or in the last year or so. The newbie who keeps wondering why all of their stock picks are "losers." I'm sure they're not all losers.

Simply put: by reading this, you will learn how to turn a little money into a lot of dough, surely more than 400 extra bucks; this book can teach you how to do that. Others promise you unrealistic money, but not this one; this is money you can somewhat easily get, and in a short amount of time too. It will take some learning from technical analysts, a bit of chart-reading, and a bunch of other stuff that we'll cover in this book. It sounds cooler (especially on TV and in movies) than what it really is, and it may even seem difficult to some. But it isn't. Once you get the hang of paying yourself first—and knowing why you should—the rest is a piece of cake. You contribute to this great economy as a consumer "spender." Isn't time for you to get some "pay-back?"

This Book is for Everyone...Truly

I'm hoping my daughters, grandsons, nieces, nephews, and the rest of the youth in the world will get a hold of this book because they "get" it faster and have all the time in the world to adopt the contrarian lifestyle. (Yes, I do use some colorful language, but it's nothing kids don't use today. I'm certainly that big kid. Plus, I have a license for my language. It's a SAG/AFTRA card ...that's my license. I've been a professional stand-up comic for most of my career. You've probably caught me on something and didn't know it. Stand-up, sitcoms, commercials, dramas or in some movie...see for yourself at www.yulspencer.com.) There are many amazing and wonderfully written books out there about the financial system that are designed only for the fortunate. Those books are informative, educational, inspiring but they will never be read by the people that really need to read them. Why? The language. I believe it's time for that highfalutin language to be tamed. So, I'm going to give it a shot in this series. The Wall Street-Smarts Series. This series will be "sucka repellent" for the main-street investor with street-smarts. We'll chop it up more about that later.

The objective of using this language is for the benefit of future generations that might profit from their own contributions to society even at the most meager level. Even those with lesser than most still contribute in a big way. They still go to the hospitals. They still love and they still buy toilet paper. We're the *contributing consumer* that needs love and money too.

By my count, adding up the population who don't even have $400 in savings or for anything extra in their lives, along with all the others I've mentioned so far (the youth, my grandchildren), this information could help almost everybody. Except, of course, for the "professional investor" (I kid the professionals; I'm sure we can be of some help to ya).

(In all honesty, remember that when you register your brokerage account, you

 will register as a "non-professional" because the non's get to take profits from the pros. #Lol)

Some readers who used to trade and invest back in the day got blown out because they didn't really understand the game or never figured out that it *is* a game and that they didn't possess any "game" themselves to start with. So they got played, and now all they know how to do is "save" a bunch of cash (by owning a home, boat, jewelry, etc.). And now that cash doesn't go to work for you anymore; it just sits in a bank paying you nothing. This book could help resurrect you.

It's got "game." #Fearof2008

Today, my friends, it's a whole new playing field out there. Since the introduction of high-speed internet,  you get to run your own game within the game "tick by tick" if you want to.

Speaking of high-speed internet, you can run this game from anywhere with internet access. The best part about this gig is having money all the time and the commute. My commute is walking down the hall from my bedroom to my office. But the even cooler thing is having liquid cash on hand (much more than $400 on any given day), and you're the one who gets to push the buttons. Now that's cool. If I could make a prediction here after the spread of the "rona" virus (covid19) I think even Wall Street traders who run teams will be working from their homes on a more permanent basis like us. It just won't be as much fun and they still will have to answer to supervisors and trade for their clients. It's not what we do. We're like that kid Kevin in *Home Alone* we do what we want to and stay paid. It should at the very least create some great volatility for us the non-professionals considering it will take a few years for them to get adjusted to working from home. We're used to it. It's another small edge but edges can benefit the investor who has it.

"The 400" is what I call us.

I was inspired to write this for several reasons. For starters, many of my

 colleagues at my age had no "real" money. I was backstage once with some well-known names in the biz, as they say, and I asked, "Who in this room has ten K cash? Right-now cash? Fu**-you cash?" And none of them could claim or prove that they had that kind of cash on them now in the moment.

So, I said to myself, *Next time I ask that question out loud or in my head, the answer will be me.* Whatever it took, I was going to learn how to get this money...legally. #Power

We were comedians and actors all living this high life because of who we were and what we did on stage or camera, but not many of us were liquid or had any money saved. Yeah, almost all of us had fancy cars and houses, some flash cash but no "real" cash on hand or in land. *What good is it to be a star at anything and you don't have access to a "minimum" of thousands of fu**-you dollars?*

Now don't misunderstand me. There were the celebs and then there were the stars. Most of the stars had money, but not all 'em knew how to manage their paper. Many of them didn't. I'm not getting into naming names, but I knew many stars and when it came to the money they couldn't shine. I've sat in the cars with some 'em while we cried about their losses. Well, they were crying. I was listening and being supportive and learning. #Peepingthegame

The answer is that the benefit of having a celeb and star status is that most folks think you do have access to that kind of cash, so they give you shit for free. It's true that the more money people think you have, the more stuff they give you for free. Huge debt is created the same way; the greater your status in the world, the more debt lenders allow you to hold onto. How wild is that, and you wonder why the rich can stay rich?

Anyway, after contemplating the lifestyle that I was a part of, I wanted to take back control of my finances. I wanted to determine where and how my money comes to me and let the show biz cash "catch up to me" when it can. #Residuals

If you're someone with great knowledge and education and your life is in full contrast with mine, this book will probably be of little help to you. You know too much to take me seriously, so you can throw this masterpiece of literature away…or, better yet, please consider giving it to someone you think might want to be, at minimum, a thousandaire, or at least have more than $400 extra when needed. Thanks; just because you're brilliant doesn't mean you can't still be kind to the lesser of us. I want this piece to go underground or be like an undercover book that falls into the hands of "suckers," a.k.a. the "participants" (non-professionals) in the market. You know that's what the Wall Street fools call us, right? If that don't get ya riled up, I got nothing.

They say these unkind things about hard-working Americans from their fancy clubs and offices a.k.a. the C-suite. I know this because I've been in there with them, and again, I think to myself, *If they said that crap on the "real" streets, they'd get their Ivy League asses whupped, most of 'em.* Not all of the elites are fu**ers calling us suckers; some understand the value of all participants. Some of 'em are tough guys, but I'm just saying, I don't think many of them would last a night on the block in D.C., Oakland, the Bronx, the South Side of Chicago or even in rural America in places like Granger, Texas.

I think you get my point, yes? You likely have more edge, balls, nerves of steel, and emotional discipline than most of these so-called alpha males/females with their eight-figure incomes and eight college degrees. With their big talk and fancy numbers that go over the average American's head intentionally. These are the men and women who call thousandaires suckers. We're also known as "dumb money," and they are considered the "smart money."

I have no beefs with anyone, but I'm aware of everyone, and you the reader should be too. You should know who you're buying and selling alongside and what they think of you. It's in your favor to know that they're not out to help you. It's an edge. The bankstas, institutions, hedge funds and all the "market-makers" want to see you lose so they can win. Makes sense? It's the game - The Wall Street Game. It's their sole purpose and job to take your money and it's your job to take theirs. No one makes money on Wall Street. The mint makes money. Corporations make money. Investors, traders and speculators, we "take" the money and add it to our P&L (profit and loss column) when the market gives it to us. We're "money-takers" not money makers. I didn't compound any interest or pay myself any dividends.

The market does all of that for us. It's all how you think about this sh** your perception you can complicate it, or you can get yours. It's why I love it. It's a money-making machine... The markets that is. You're going to hear a lot 'bout the "Bears and the Bulls" not the sports teams. #Chicago

You'll learn more about them in this series, but I just wanted to give you a heads up that we're both and we're neither. What I aim for is to be profitable as I can be. No matter what direction the market is headed into. Up or down. I let all of you play the game and I focus on winning it—letting the game come to me. #LastDance

Positive people like myself always believing that the American economy will remain profitable for decades to come at least for my lifetime are for the most part the "Bulls" and those who would believe the opposite are the "Bears". This candid knowledge about who's, who with no chaser could be considered an edge. Everyone sooner or later develops an edge. One of mines is to know who the players are.

Nevertheless, I'm truly making a point for the ninety-nine percent, the citizens who would let all that fancy noise (talk) and fancy people stop them from getting what they can out of the market. Because when you start listening to the noise of these people, you will start doubting your own limited abilities. These doubts will rise to the surface of your thinking of yourself. You will say once or twice, *I'm not smart enough,* but I have really great news for you: to get these thousands, you don't have to be a genius. A limited education can still take a profit—street-smarts.

I don't know why these "high rollers" can't play it straight. Greed, I guess. Power, maybe, but I don't want that to keep hard-working people out of the game. Let them be crazy while you save and increase your paper. Fu** them; it's time for you to learn you can get yours too. You don't need what they have or want what they need. You only need what you need.

Who Am I?

Before we go any further, you may be wondering, who is this Yul Spencer guy? I will admit, I am a truly blessed person, a walking miracle. I've been shot, ran over by an undercover vehicle, and addicted to a lot of bad shit. I'll leave it at that for now, because this is not a self-help book per se, though your personality, character, and emotions do play a big part in anyone becoming a successful investor/trader on these stock exchanges around the world. This "Wall St. Game" isn't for the weak of heart or the person who beats up on themselves all day. My blessings come from my supportive loved ones in my life.

Now, I want to jump out in front of the fact that I'm not from "Wall Street;" I'm sure you've guessed that by now with my intro. But let me be clear: while growing up, I was never made aware that I could even apply to an Ivy League school, so I never went to one. This should put you at ease a bit and be somewhat of a relief, I hope.

I won't be talking above anyone's head, that's for sure, but if you've never grown up a survivor on the "real streets" in this country, I might write something you've never heard related to the stock market before. It's because my education started in them real streets, though I did later get a scholarship to go to San Jose State University (SJSU), where I stayed for two-and-a-half years. During that time, I met my soon-to-be-ex-wife of eleven years. (Side note: why do we call our ex's "ex's" when they should be "y's"... as in *why* did we get married? Why's she still callin' me? Why she keep asking me for money? Why, why, why?)

Back to SJSU. My major was in Business Administration, but I also learned to excel in the "black market" (pharmaceuticals). I'm sure that's why I never finished at SJSU, though I did go back to college to study Theater Arts at Laney College in Oakland, CA. So, I went to college. I'm not a complete dummy, but I'm not the sharpest knife in the drawer either. If I tell the complete truth here, I entered college after being locked up for my entire juvenile life. I got the credits to get into college while in lock up! After my release, I entered college and turned the place out giving parties and running an entirely different game. I imagine I'm a lot like you. I'm just messing with you, but I think what separates us from some of the Wall Street folks is that we still live in the real-world. Which I think gives us the "dumb-money" an edge. Let me add here some of these Wall Street folks are real gangstas too. Don't get it twisted. My first education started off in the "real" streets in Oakland, CA, and throughout the Bay Area among drug dealers, pimps, and club owners. See, a different kind of gangsta.

It was a different market, but a market, nonetheless. The psychological game and emotional discipline it took to succeed on them streets had a great impact on the way I handle "risk" today. As a matter of fact, the real streets took it to another level. For example, if you found yourself "short" (short of this day's take), there was no nice margin call from your broker or brokerage firm asking you to pay up before the end of the day. In the real streets, you got shot or beaten down. So, *risk* for me is fractal; it's stuck in my brain over and over, and I know it can meet with serious consequences.

This is probably why I think of my trading style as "highly adaptable," making risk management the dominant focus in my strategy. *How much can I afford to lose?* is one of the first questions I ask myself before entering a trade or an investment or committing more capital to my fund. Whatever that answer is, I go with it. I have a standard practice of allocating only 2.5 percent of my total capital toward any trade. Investments could be as high as 5 percent, and then I adapt. I can hear some of the voices reading this right now (I can, I hear you) saying, "Sh**, I can't lose **no** money." #NeverLose

Nevertheless, the reality is that every day you are already losing all you've earned and can't save. So was I before I found out how to make money into more money. Old Skool is what I am. I guess a busta would say, but without the loved ones in my life and a belief in the bigger me, I wouldn't have the support to earn a living this way in the markets. If you're alone and you get good at trading, you won't be alone for long, and you want to be around those who support what you do. It will make all the difference in why you do what you are doing. Did I say trading was easy? Believe me, it is, and it isn't, but it's worth it.

I believe this book will help many become thousandaires. That's my ultimate intention for writing this, because becoming a thousandaire has to come before all the other "aires" (millionaire, billionaire, etc.). You must learn to crawl before you walk and then run, as my granddaddy would say when we were children. My core belief is that this knowledge can add wealth to the lives of all Americans to put an end to "broke-ness." Everything in life has a process, and trading on the stock exchange is no different. You must trust it, and you must trust ***you***. You will learn, as the great prophet Grace Jones sang years ago, "I may not be perfect, but I'm perfect for you." #StockMarket

SENSE OF URGENCY
$400 = 911

FOUR HUNDRED DOLLARS EQUALS NINE-ONE-ONE. You might say that's bad math. But is it? The average person standing, sitting, or even lying next to you doesn't have $400 extra to their name. That equals a clear 911 emergency.

You know the television show *Let's Make a Deal* with my man Wayne Brady? That show is "bananas" because the audience has to be dressed up like bananas (it's required). This televised swap meet shows what folks will do for a lil' money. Four hundred dollars is nothing for Wayne; he pulls that out of his pockets every day. It's more like $500 to $1500, and the folks in the crazy outfits lose their damn minds for 500 extra bucks and to be on TV, which I believe is the real win for the audiences that go to game shows. It can't be the money, and certainly not for a profit. Think about what those folks had to do to get that money: pick out some embarrassing, nutty outfit that would get noticed by producers, book a hotel, fly to L.A., take time off from work because they shoot those shows during the weekdays. Maybe get a babysitter to throw into the "sunk cost." Now, I'm just estimating by trips I have taken, but that's probably a sunk cost of let's say $3,000 to receive—and I'm saying this is the highest of probabilities—nothing (zero). Now, I know this most likely was an event included in their Hollywood vacation, but the point here is that in this book, you will learn how to make extra money for yourself over and over again in the stock market and never ever be required to wear a "chicken suit" (unless that's your thing, of course).

So, what's the "sense of urgency," you say? We've already talked about the average American not having $400 extra cash to their names. Now your car broke down and you can't get to work? You're stuck without a safety net. Most Americans have no money for life's little obstacles that pop up. Most of us can't even get together with each other on the regular because of money (pre-corona). Quiet as kept the new rules help broke people stay broke. Now we shouldn't get together because someone might be sick not just broke. #Rona

Besides, why be an average American anymore, when we can be above average quite easily? Together, you, me, we can plug a hole in this poverty.

When I heard the stat about most Americans not having $400 to their name, I couldn't believe it was that bad for everyone. I dropped my head and said, *I have to share what I've learned already with everyone and anyone who will listen!* How is it possible that everyone doesn't know about where to "rob the rich" legally? How do they not know where all the rich people park their money? And how do they not know in "these days" they're allowed to take it (the money) if they're willing to learn how? Why doesn't the average broke American know this, or why hasn't it been clearly explained to the public in such a simplistic way that they get it? For that reason, the birth of this book series had to happen.

I entitled my next book *Turning Losers into Winners* because if you're an honest (and I use the word loosely) swing, day, or long-term trader or investor, you know that many times, when a trade starts out, it's jumped on by the financial news and other media outlets and begins to be perceived as a loser first before they become winners. When you see your stock falling on the chart because of "general semantics" (google it) used in the media or because you just made a bad entry (bought in at the top), *you think what they want you to think:* that it's a loser. It's usually the highest probability after you've done all the work, hunted your favorite stock down to its lowest base price you thought, and put on a trade just to watch it go against you, down even lower.

I'm laughing inside while I'm writing this, but I can't help it because it happens a lot. This occurs so much that it turns some of the strongest-minded people into sufferers of the Dow, and many have quit because they can't take a simple draw-down, pull-back, dip; whatever you want to call it, it all amounts to the same thing: buying losers. Many new traders wonder if it's the HFT's (high frequency traders) fault or the algos (algorithms), or maybe it's the "market makers." Naw, it's a short squeeze. What the hell is that? Who the fu** knows, but it happens all the time. We have to say to ourselves what that dude Jim Cramer on *Mad Money* hollas at the Fed about: "You know nothing!"

. . .

We know nothing; we know only what we're capable of finding out. #NoWorries

---

> It's not necessary for us to know everything. They don't know everything either. Nobody knows everything. Most of us know nothing! #Equal

---

However, "turning losers into winners" can have a broad meaning. I could be writing about oneself or talking about equities/stocks and the mean reversion (definitely google the mean reversion).

My primary focus will be on the equities/stocks and the "mean" making you money. So, as you grasp how to use your Wall Street-Smarts, you'll learn how to become a consistently profitable investor/trader in this market. It's what I've learned to do with not only stocks but my everyday life. "All I do nowadays is win, win, win, no matter what, money on mind, I can never get enough." #DJKhaled

The days you don't feel like a winner which shouldn't last long you can pivot to being a learner, a student of the game. Which can assure you succeed at winning.

See, it wasn't enough for me to learn from the actors backstage that big-shot celebrities didn't have $10K on hand. Hearing that the average American doesn't even have $400, that means half this country is "financially handicapped" with no parking spots! #Crucial

It really chaps my ass! I learned that saying in Texas, "it chaps my ass." So, let me begin with the word "patience," because it will become the most important word for the at-home hedge fund manager. I coined that phrase myself "the at-home-hedge fund manager." Fortunately, it's something you can learn. If you don't have a lot of patience now, it's okay as the saying goes, there's no way you can eat an entire "Hometown Buffet" in one sitting. That is the saying right? But bit by bit or bite by bite, you could eat the entire buffet in due time. Please be patient with yourself and give yourself time to learn the game using your own "street-smarts." Before you know it, you're a thousandaire and making and having more money than the person probably standing next to you. You ever heard that story about not having to be the fastest runner in a group of people trying to escape something horrifying? You just have to be faster than the person next to you. It's kind of like that. I'm not suggesting that we're all going to make a fortune in the stock market. I'm suggesting that we don't have less than four hundred dollars to our names on any given day. Get that extra and keep that extra growing 'til you have more than enough for you. That's all that matters. What someone else has or is doing is not our business unless we use it as motivation or education in some ways. Other than that, you do you and I'll do me.

I dislike very much not being able to do something for someone or myself because I lack the money to do it. That pisses me off, and if you get that, then you will do what it takes to take control of your financial future. Please understand, I'm talking to all human beings with a pulse, a driver's license number, and whole lot of desire to learn. I said nothing about money. It's the desire to learn about money, the economy and how it actually works that gets you paid. The money will come when the desire to learn how to get it is great. As you read on, you'll learn that less money is more, at the beginning stages anyhow.

You might not like what you've read so far, because I know when I read a book on trading or about a trader, I'm like, *Come on man, let's get to the trading methods*. Then, after I've read their book, I realize the story was just as important as learning the author's methods. It's about the lessons you remember when you finally put on a trade and then you ask yourself, *What did that author say about drawdowns?* "Ah, that's right, they shared that story. I remember now!" And if you remember in time, you probably turned a losing trade into a winner.

I knew I needed to share this information, but I didn't want to get on stage talking about this stuff.

(Though I do plan on being in a movie about finance in the future...but I digress.) Nevertheless, there had to be a better way to share with Americans as soon as possible that they can and should have at least a thousandaire lifestyle.

So, spreading the word about one of the last and greatest legal American businesses you can get into for virtually zero down—and get rich too, if that's your desire—is my new "call to duty." If you're willing to follow your own rules, you can learn to take money—I re-emphasis *legally*—every day from the wealthiest economy and people on the planet. You are welcome to play. It's your right. Some say it's a sin to be poor ("sin" meaning "error"). I agree. And guess what? It doesn't matter what kind of American you are, regardless of race, religion, or sex, none of the things that get us into trouble when we have to show up in person matter in the stock market. You can be a 400-pound man sitting on the edge of a bed...let me stop. If your sense of humor is still intact, let's continue. On a side-note when the "rona" virus hit the world, I was already working from home. It was a huge blessing to have an at-home hedge fund already kicking out paper. I had my own pandemic plan already in place and didn't even know it 'til I needed it.

In the #WallStGame, you're invisible, we're invisible; yeah, we're like actual "invisible" men and women taking money from the visible. No one knows it's you. No one who matters anyways knows it's you who just made that trade or investment. Believe it or not that's not what you'll hear from an undisciplined trader full of anger and vigor. Some of them will swear up and down that some lil' man is in their computers, stealing and shorting all their great trades. But the truth is that nobody knows it's you or your computer even, so please don't throw your wireless keyboard across the room, busting all three of your brand-new curve screens. (Yes, I did that sh**.) It's only you, the thousandaire, so be really aware and understand that the SEC does not publicly publish your trades (game recognizes game) in the *Wall Street Journal*, but they do publish the millionaires, billionaires, and trillion-dollar corporations buying back their own stock at noteworthy prices. Which is valuable intel/data for the savvy at-home thousandaire who takes that trade as well or makes an investment.

. . .

Nobody knows it's you, but you know it's them. This could be considered an edge if you are a consumer of much data. When you're an at-home hedge fund manager, interpreting data is crucial. If you're as street savvy as I am, you'll "get" that most of these people on TV, social media, podcasts, and any other way they can get to ya are straight up lying. Sure, they call it "semantics" meaning they're giving out bad advice or creating false narratives to create a constant wheel of buyers and sellers. It's a trip how bullshit is rationalized to be legal talk. Check out my man's book *Winning The Mental Game on Wall Street* by John Magee. They use a lot of fancy words to bullshit you legally when really, they don't know much more than you do; they just sound like they do. Every once in a while, they find someone who actually does know what they're doing. Me, I see it all as lies that don't fit my objectives or strategy. When you know someone is lying to you, what do you do? Well, what I do is let them lie, and then I do whatever is the opposite of what they're lying about. If they say it's time to buy but that's not in line with my strategy or objective, I'll prepare to sell and so on. You have to be sharp in determining whose FOS (full of sh**)

and who isn't, so you'll hear quite a bit to do your own due diligence when researching stocks. I would say that is a really good idea. Doing the work yourself offers a certain MOS (margin of safety) to every buy you make. It creates a confidence that won't allow you to be easily scared out of your positions. According to American investor and mutual fund manager Peter Lynch, "the key to making money in stocks is not to get scared out of them." I keep that quote in a frame on a wall just above my buy and sell screen.

You will be amazed at what some of these alphas get degrees in and how determined these really smart people are at beating this market or just making all the cash they can without you. However, your objectives will never line up with theirs, so don't worry about it. It's mind-boggling and again discouraging to the average retail investor. Don't you let it get you down. I don't know how or why it's legal to outright lie to the American people about the direction of the market, growth, or valuations of different stocks on public forums, but apparently it is. And then "they" turn around and call it something else, like "falsehoods" or "half-truths." It's still lying, and in the real streets, a lie is a lie. Once the at-home investors wrap their heads around it and shut it down, you'll be on the other side of the trade making profits. What you know, you know, and what you don't know, you don't know, so don't worry about acting like you do. Just get YOUR money. "Get your money. Get your money." #ChildishGambino

And beware of quants and algos (algorithms), who don't sound like very nice people, but that's because they're not people at all; they're not even human. Okay. Quants are human. They just don't do human sh**. They're scientists. It's above my pay grade and probably yours. A fu**ing quant can't be good for normal human participants. I kid the quants. These gals and guys are brilliant. I repeat, they're scientists. We can't compete, but they do exist, and the HFT (high fu**ing frequency trading) folks have the machines programmed to trade every tick and pip in a nanosecond. A fu**ing fly couldn't catch these trades, they're so tiny, swift, and mighty (in volume).

Please take some time to study all this technical stuff. You can spend time being your own research team, because risk management trading allows a lot of reading time. I suggest you get familiar with what's out there if only for the reason of being aware; believe me, we can't compete, nor do we have to. But awareness gives you an "edge." #WallStSmarts

They actually help us get those thousands by creating so much volatility in the market. Big up and down movements. $VIX

And because they don't know who we are, they don't know who's on the other side of the trade. Which gives you the edge if you can learn to "wait for it" and have the steely patience to take the big profits. If you can master yourself, you'll always have thousands on the weekend instead of, well, let's say not even $400, according to the folks who take these polls.

You know by now that really bothers me, so let me keep typing. When I ask the universe if this piece of literature will reach the folks that it must, I'm encouraged that this won't just be another book about traders but a book that made many thousandaires out of traders. #FIRE

And that it will catch those who have been on the fence about trading or investing in themselves and *our* great American economy. I believe the game I'm spittin' here can help anyone overcome themselves and the market. Because if this author can do it, anyone can. We all have read the best of the best trading and investing books and yet have we read one that puts emphasis on just having extra money, on being a thousandaire? No, we have not. #Profitable

However, the big talkers of finance seem to shame and look down on the thousandaire, like having thousands of dollars won't make you a name (or popular). What if you preferred not to have a name on Wall Street but rather to have money in your purse and wallet? Trust me, I had a name and not much money, and that sh** ain't fulfilling at all. But $13K liquid on any given day means we can do more for ourselves, our families, and the people and causes we love. Don't let anyone make you feel bad because you only have $50K to fu** off.

First lesson in equities will be to begin training your mind to think in the highest of probabilities and to know that in most cases what zigs, zags. We'll go deeper into this in the following chapters.

I've helped some friends, family, and other likeminded people, to get their own brokerage accounts to meet their own personal objectives. I have managed some small accounts to improve my own skills and help them to increase their capital until they've saved enough money to open their own accounts. It makes you feel good to help someone else get theirs. #PayItForward

Alright, the next step is to know your objectives. Why are you doing this? To save for something specifically, have an extra income, or just enjoy more spending money? Do you want to make this your life work or just add to your life? Could it be you're trying to prove you're the sharpest knife in the drawer? The latter is assured to fail, but knowing your objectives is half your battle. Really, it is, and you must get this! As an at-home thousandaire, it will help you to remain emotionally disciplined and make you money. Knowing your objectives for trading is critical. #BelieveMe

Oh, I can't wait to share with you about losses. MY GOODNESS, so much focus on losing in these markets, the *noise* of the market, including these lying ass analysts. Oh, forgive me, the "misleading" analysts, so-called gurus, and the rude short sellers and their cartels. But here's the truth: losses are for day traders, option guys, and speculators, not us thousandaires. Believing otherwise is just downright ruinous for many who follow these guys and gals. I'm personally disgusted by these men and women who are paid to cause hard-working Americans to lose their money to the rich by spinning one speculation story after another, they could be making them winners instead. Or, how 'bout they just stay out of the way altogether and quit hurting the middle class? Just don't say anything.

Sorry, that's not the way it is in the markets. It's like they say in *Trading Places*: "eat or be eaten." I like to eat, and I know you do too, so let's continue on to see how we keep doing that. We'll discuss losses in further detail in upcoming chapters, but just know for now that when you know what you want, the rest is a piece of cake.

There is a lot of consuming work in front of you; it's true that learning about how your money works in this industry can suck up some time but are you too busy to learn how to pay yourself? You have to ask yourself that question. Learning about investments and the economy is an all-consuming animal, so I hope you love numbers and money like I do. If so, then you'll never be bored. Making money will (and should) be fun. Though I heard a quote not long ago from one of the ol' kats in the game George Soros. It went "If investing is entertaining, if you're having fun, you're probably not making any money. Good investing is boring." The point about good investing being boring is somewhat true (due diligence, research) but that doesn't mean you have to be boring and broke. I'm taking the money I command. Not the money a dude like Soros is taking from the markets. I think it's important for those of us in the game to remember just because someone is richer than you doesn't make him smarter than you. It makes them richer. I've seen other traders post these quotes from the legends in the game on social media as if they adhere to the meanings as if they feel the same way George or Warren does. As if they were trader law in some way. You will need to take everything you hear or read especially on social media not at its word. You have to be the "sponge" soak up the mess-age and squeeze out the excess. Your story will never be their story. It's time we all write our own stories. #Truedat

If you're not having fun, it's because you probably are boring but that's okay and if you're capable of having fun you can still be consistently profitable. #Serious

Once you learn the importance of having your own fund and begin enjoying never being broke because of you, you'll kick yourself for not learning sooner. Well, maybe that's just me. As I'm writing this book, I'm still building my own account to six figures…but I'm on my way. That's why I'm passing on what I've learned so far now and it's why I feel the "sense of urgency" to do it. I couldn't wait 'til I'm a billionaire to write this book. Shoot only God knows how long that will take... if ever! But I knew if tried to wait to be rich first to write these books I'd be keeping valued data to myself that I know for sure could help many people immediately. When I saw that $400 crisis headline, I knew at that moment someone had to put the word out, and so it looks like that someone is me.

I may never become a millionaire or billionaire trading, and you might not either; we might obtain ours in some other way (if that's even what you want), but should that stop us from enjoying a pathway there and having liquid cash on hand in the meantime? And if we do obtain millions in some other way, we now have a place to put it... in our funds. An acting friend of mine used to say starving actors, actually starve. It's true.

What I'm suggesting is believable and doable within a few years. Believe me, letting go of this crazy notion that we're all going to be big investors like Buffett, Icahn, Dalio, or any of these ol' kats is not likely to happen. It's something you don't have to think about because you don't invest like they invest; their objectives are not your objectives, and we don't have their kind of cash in the first place. Let them be your guide, but not your clone. Don't worry about being like "Mike;" it's never going to happen, but you *can* be like you and me and live life as a thousandaire before deciding to move higher. "Crawl before you walk," another one of my Granddaddy's sayings when we were kids. Or you might not want to go higher, and you may like your life flying below the radar. #WallStSmarts

What I'm writing about is achievable, not these "pie in the sky" books where everybody can be a billionaire. That's not true for many reasons, the main one being that many of you don't really want to be billionaires and wouldn't know what to do if it happened to you. So, stop thinking about trading like you're "The Wolf of Wall Street" and instead be cool, stay calm, and collect these thousands by taking the money from the very billionaires we like to revere. "KEEP CALM AND TAKE YOUR MONEY."

. . .

Having more than enough money is enough for many of us, but public pressure and finance gurus and their autobiographies put out the idea that we can't do this for ourselves unless we're doing it to become millionaires or billionaires. That isn't true, but so many would-be investors give up even trying because having thousands isn't a worthy goal. I sh** you not. Bottom line, what I'm writing about can be done for all Americans with a driver's license number and some street smarts.

OBJECTIVES

INVESTING BEGINS with what might be a new discipline for many of you, and that is *saving money and knowing your objectives for investing at the same time*. I've discovered that many would-be investors found out early in life that saving money in a usual bank account is no fun and of no real benefit. And because most people don't get much out of doing it, they are discouraged from saving. You can't keep up with it, because life keeps charging you a grip to stay here.

One of the positives of this new era has been all these apps that help would-be investors round off spending cash and save money. The depositors feel like they are getting something out of it. That's the point of being an investor: you put your money into something, and more money comes out. It's like alchemy. (Speaking of, if you haven't read the book *The Alchemist*, you should add it to your reading list now...love that book.) One of the best explanations for owning a gun is in that book. The English dude traveling with the seeker of the Alchemist told the kid who asks why do you have a gun? He replied, "It helps me trust people." I thought that was insightful.

I like the idea of gathering enough knowledge to turn money into more money. And that is always my objective, coinciding with saving money simultaneously while maximizing my cash balance. You can say these three are my primary objectives, and by knowing my primary objectives, I can stay in my lane and allocate risk based on that knowledge. I never have to go overboard on any trade. This is why knowing your objectives is literally half your battle and protects your money with a MOS (margin of safety). When you're not clear about your objectives and you enter the market all willy-nilly, you'll get eaten up. Well, your money will, anyway.

. . .

How do we determine our objectives? Well, that could take a minute or two of just sitting alone, being still, and pondering in your mind what you want to achieve. Sharing this with you reminds me of a time I was at a "roast" for Magic Earvin Johnson Jr. at the Kodak Theater in Hollywood, CA. And someone in the green room asked him before going out on stage how he achieved so much wealth? And he spoke to all of us in the room and shared that most people especially "our" people, but that people in general have the inability to remain "still" long enough to receive the blessings they been dreaming of. Be Still.

Once you've locked in your objectives you can allow yourself to upgrade them along the way. You will see you've created a template to be successful. If you're not one to break your *own rules*, you can profit faster and sooner than traders who haven't mapped out their objectives. They may not know how they will react when the market opens, but those of us who know our objectives know exactly how we will react most of the time. I say "most of the time" because adaptability is also a tool, a skill, even. Really, if you remember I wrote earlier when I was backstage with my fellow comics and actors that the next time I asked who had fu** you money of let's say ten grand it was going to be me. And today I can gladly say that it is me. Truly that was my first objective to always have ten grand on hand. And anything that interferes with that objective I must let go of even if the trade is favorable at the time. #Objectives

You'll need to adapt quickly to changes in the market and adapting will become second nature to most of you. When you have your objectives in place, adapting will be effortless. If you haven't done this yet, please, as we go deeper into this joint, think about doing it before your next trading day. It will make all the difference in your mind and body while investing. The market has a way of rewarding those who aren't desperate to win. It's like the lazier you are once you put on your trade, the more the market rewards you. Believe me, there is a lot of nap-taking for me during the trading hours, with alerts set to go off when stocks go up or down. When you have your objectives in place, you can chill and watch. You can observe your money making you money. I know you must be thinking, *Is this guy on something or onto something?* I'm sharing my experience as a thousandaire and an at-home hedge fund dude. I'm not in some fancy office overlooking Broad St. in New York. Instead, most of us are in an office inside our fancy houses, looking out the window at whatever view nature provides for us. Now, I tease the short sellers, because I imagine them all in a basement somewhere; that just makes sense to me. I'm laughing again just thinking about it.

Nevertheless, I want to make it clear to you what to prepare for, otherwise, there are special guru teachers you can sign up with who will try to mold you into some insane, overwhelmed gambler. All that extra stuff is gambling; it's certainly not investing. *We will remain focused on the would-be investor and trader who thought they could never make money in the market or that the market wasn't for them.* I'm here to share with them they may be wrong. Less than 50 percent of Americans are even aware of how to earn money from the market; it has intimidated the average American intentionally to keep you out and the rich in, getting richer without you. You might think I'm obsessed with this objective thing but think about it: once you know what you want, someone can't easily throw you off your game with theirs. They have their strategy fu**ed up, so they want your strategy fu**ed up. Game must recognize game. It's their intention to throw you off of yours and out of the markets. So, we lose and they win.

Some people do well around others, but those of us who are at home getting these thousands have a more satisfying days not answering to anyone else. We are the bosses of us, and as long as we are meeting our own objectives (not those of some billionaire) every day, I'm good being a thousandaire flying under the radar.

Back to the topic at hand. I keep my objectives written on a 3x5" card on my desk. It reads: "I saved money, I made money, I did not lose any money, I traded well." These are my daily objectives. You will have as many as you need daily, monthly, annually, and forevermore. Whatever your life will look like as an investor/trader, these objectives will keep you topside. Remember, earlier in my intro I said that you won't ever become a millionaire without becoming a thousandaire first (Excluding an inheritance or the lotto). Everything is a process. We plant the seed, and we wait for the thing to grow.

GREATER FOOLS CREATE MOS
(MARGIN OF SAFETY)

OTHER TRADERS you've read about have formulas; I have a whole lot of common sense and street smarts, which makes me adaptive to almost anything. The greater fool is the fool greater than you. There's always someone who is more foolish than you in the markets and you can rely on that fool to help you create a margin of safety. It's only one factor too many but it's reliable in my experience. Growing up surviving instead of living creates a natural edge. (You know it's tough to bullshit a bullshitter, right?) When it comes to these markets, not much scares me.

. . .

We'll talk later when I'm trading millions, but I believe once you learn how to trade, it's actually easier with millions than with hundreds or thousands of dollars coupled with the lack of experience we all possess when we begin. That's why I shared with you at the beginning of this book that "less is more;" once you learn what you're doing, you can allocate more and more money.

To begin with, I have no intentions of beating these markets ever. On the real streets, take my word for it, I know what happens to people who like to beat things. It's not a good look. The same mindset and consequences are in the market, and you will lose. In the streets, the police come to get you and put you away; in the market, you can lose money, but you can always make it up again. It's not fatal like in the real streets. Now, thieves and greedy mf's get caught on Wall Street all the time, we know this, but none of them will ever read this book. By the time any of them could read this book, it'd be too late. They would probably be checking it out of the prison library. On the real streets, you could lose your life, go to prison, or lose a part of your body and have to live with the scars. I have a few. I've gotta gunshot wound and a few knife cuts and a scar from being burned with a hot light bulb. I share this with you so you can get it through your head that no one runs you but you in these markets, and no one's going to shoot you if you get a trade wrong.

The first thing to realize is that there will always be a greater fool than you to pay a higher price for a stock you bought too high. That isn't the point; the point is what you paid for it, and that sooner or later a greater fool will come along and pay more than you had to. (If you've done your homework, you'll find out how true this is.) Now, how long you can wait for that greater fool is up to you. Your threshold isn't mine, and mine isn't yours. When I put on trade or make an investment, I'm thinking forever. Not just "long" but forever, because I choose to invest and not day trade (But that's me. You do you.) You must develop "Kevlar" skin metaphorically, of course. On the streets, we had the "vests" for real. For real. You'll need the emotional discipline to win, and before you know it, that greater fool will appear. Also, you should know that most of the time (highest probabilities), what goes up comes down, and what goes down can come up again. You just have to have done the due diligence and have the patience, a MOS, and an excellent ability to shut out the "noise." This is what I call "Wall St. Smarts" or "Wall St. Game;" so many claim they have game, but they don't know the game. Of course, you have heard the wise ol' adage to buy low and sell high? IT STILL WORKS! IT'S AN UNDEFEATED METHOD.

The "noise" will tell you it's a harder thing to do than to say. I'm telling you they're lying their asses off. If you become a good hunter, learn to stalk stocks, and put in some stake-out time, you will learn through your own experience and patience that they're lying to you. It happens all the time. Remember "the most interesting man" commercials? I'd like to make one with this line for the financial news: (imagine his voice in your head.) "Buy low and sell high my friends, and don't let anyone tell you otherwise." A new "most interesting man" on Wall St.

Reading charts and candlesticks is very helpful, so learn to do that stuff online too. You know what I'm going to suggest by now: google it. So many other books teach the unknowing to sell out and lose money like it's some kind of fu**ing badge of honor. "Learn how to lose money," "put on a tight stop-loss," "never be afraid to get out of a losing trade," is all advice you hear without making things clear to the unknowing, the inexperienced. What the fu** is a losing trade? As soon as a trade goes against one of these bright, spirited new traders who're trying to upgrade their lives, they sell out and lose money. This blows holes into their trading accounts, and they never trade or invest in the stock market again. They never have control over their financial destiny and are discouraged for life. #Sad.

I would never tell anyone to lose money or to get used to losing; now, that's some crazy sh** that would get you shot where I'm from. I have to learn how to lose money out in these streets. No, we don't lose money like that, ladies and gents. On the real streets, taking a loss doesn't equate to losing it equates to learning some sh** about yourself so you can win. Same thing goes in the stock market (on Wall St.); you can drop something (a bad seed) for less to get more. That's being sagacious, and we all must learn to be sagacious in this game. I like that word sagacious look it up and never be embarrassed about what you don't know, yet. Look that stuff up.

You should also never fall in love with a stock. It's like the saying from the good prophet, the late, great Nate Dogg, who said in a song years ago, "We don't love these hoes." We traders don't fall in love with these stocks. What I'm sharing with you is to learn to "risk" the proper amount of money on any trade and then wait. Simple, right? It really is, once you know your risk tolerance, which is another required skill and a must-have.

This is all a good start, but I know you want some real complicated answer with detailed statistics and backtesting. I'm not going to waste your time on things I know you can google. You can do all that backtesting during your trading schedule for yourself. This due diligence is done on every trade, but that's just to make you think you know something. It has to be done for your own confidence. But it's why fundamentals are nicknamed "funnymentals," because they can be helpful at times but not really when determining a winning trade or investment. A greater fool, though, that's something you can count on. Once you're more familiar with the community online, at public conferences, and on TV, it's there you can physically see some of the folks on the other side of these trades. You can look them in their eyes and see a new, greater fool every day.

Also remember that we discussed patience is key to earning big in the stock market; most people lose because they lack the rock-like patience to win big. It's a lot like Vegas, where whoever can afford to play the longest wins. Unlike Vegas—where, if you're wrong, you can't take your playing cards or bet off the table (at least not without some form of punishment)—in the stock market, you can back out of your trade. You may not get all your money back, but you won't have to suffer any great losses you can't make up. And, similar to Vegas, there's always a greater fool to sit in the stool next to you.

It's human nature on the real streets; we used to say if you find a fool, you must accept him as a fool, or you become the greater fool. (I did clean that up a bit, so if anybody from the block finds themselves reading this joint, I don't want you to tweet me saying, *That's not how we say it, fool.*) I'm sure there will be some other professional investors and traders saying how they've heard all about the "greater fool" and are well aware of them and the edge they bring to the market, but they've never heard it put exactly like this. That's why *this* book had to be written. The high-class fools would never tell you about themselves, and no one likes to think he or she is the greater fool. That's why it's me writing this instead of some guy with a Wall Street reputation to protect. I'm throwing all kinds of shade on folks who don't respect the shareholders, a.k.a. "the participants," a.k.a. you, my friend, the reader. See, I find it somewhat hard to believe that anyone managing millions and billions of dollars would be interested in reading *this* book, so that's another *edge* you can keep as a gift from me. They'll never know what you know now. #Boom

Understand, they don't care about us enough to make us skeptical of the market. That's why I had to write this material before I reached my own pinnacle in this business where I'm making so much money and doing so well that the retail investor can't believe in me anymore. #JimCramer

At that point, I'd have to start sharing from a place to protect my newfound wealth, so I'm sharing this information before any of that happens. See, how wealthy I am doesn't matter in writing this book, but how experienced I am should. Appealing to those who are already wealthy is the farthest thing from my mind. Remember, I'm writing this with that American citizen in mind who doesn't even have _400 dollars_ extra to his/her name. Oh, you can chill; though I am a thousandaire, discussing your wealth in public is a tacky thing to me and still troublesome. "Game recognize game," and I'm not into attracting things in my life I don't want. I don't want any of our readers to think because some people are millionaires or billionaires that they must be smarter than most men and women on the planet. Ehhh, wrong! I've met some really stupid millionaires that I wouldn't follow to the bathroom. #Weinstein

So, you the reader can rest assured I come from where most of us come from: the school of hard knocks and butt whuppings. But don't get it wrong, I like millionaires and billionaires. I'm just saying they're not all smarter than us. Even though they are richer. #LOL

I don't want to hear any longer that so many of our neighbors can't save $400. I'm sure most of them don't even know that in this new world, they can open up an account at a brokerage firm for free. Getting into this business—because it absolutely can become a business—costs nothing, no minimum deposit to start.

I can't tell you how many folks don't understand how easy it is to get in the market and start trading and making that extra $400 over and over again. I won't suggest to anyone that they should be in the market, but *everyone should be in the market*. Nevertheless, the desire to trade and invest in your economy you helped create is a personal decision, I believe, that should not be taken lightly. What comes with money is responsibility for the money, and you'll have to learn that if you don't already know it. Handling money responsibly is also critical.

. . .

First and foremost, you've got to open your free trading account (I suggest using Fidelity.com). Then you deposit money (I recommend $1,000) in that account to start trading. I can almost hear you hollering, "But I don't have $1,000...I don't even have $400!" Right. It doesn't have to be all at once. You can open an account with zero dollars. Then you might want to skip that daily 3 lottery ticket and put that money into your free trading account and make you some real money. Or you might go bigger and save $100/week for ten weeks. You do whatever it takes: setting aside the money you work so hard for every day, dedicating those tips you get in this new gig economy. You begin the practice now of paying yourself first by putting money into that free brokerage account.

Okay, now you have done some homework; read all the books on indicators, charts, indexes, sectors, ETF's and so on (I will list some of my favorites in the back of this book); you've began getting all your objectives in mind; you have saved your $1,000 to start trading. Congratulations; you are well on your way to becoming a thousandaire! If you haven't tripped on it, you now have four hundred dollars put up for anything you want.

Let's break down the many different thought processes and phases of becoming a consistently profitable investor/trader, starting with considering market dynamics before even entering a trade or an investment. This practice is vital, but it's something I observe daily that seems to be overlooked and ignored by many participants. Marketing dynamics matter before entering a trade. What's going on in the world and the market overall. Globally, internationally, locally, etc. What's happening!

When it comes to picking the right stocks, there is such a thing as applying the hunting mentality, "staking out a stock" and understanding why buying low and selling high is so easy to do but why the noise keeps pushing participants to believe otherwise.

. . .

You might be wondering how to go about picking a company to invest in? We'll cover that but for the most part you do your homework. For me, researching and investigating corporations turned out to be a lot of fun. I like to learn about things I never knew, but that's me. For now, I want you to google all the things you commonly learn in other trader books; there's so much literature out there about strategies and methods, but you should get familiar with all of the different literature that's out there online first. Self-learning is a must, so read, read, read, and when you're tired of reading, read something else. It may sound like a lot of work, but it's worth it. Being a thousandaire is just the beginning of anything you want. It's a launching pad.

You should also be prepared to consider your risk threshold. Think about it as we go along and you learn more. Risk management is a top priority for any investor. On the real streets, you always had to have some product and lots of cash. You never had all your money in one block or in one job; you had to spread it out, playa. You had something going on at several night clubs, liquor stores, and apartment buildings. You never put all your business on display in one spot. Certain fellas on the block thought they were so cold that they could protect their holdings on one block, until that one block got shot up and the police shut it down, rolling squad cars by there on a regular. My man was shut down instantly and had to gather his losses and open up somewhere else. You always had to be ready to pay for a better deal or buy up whatever can make you more money that day and replace any losses before you got shot. So, holding cash, having cash was absolutely crucial, even if you had to go into your own personal bankroll to cover any potential losses and avoid harm to your life. The rule here is to always have some cash. Cash may not be King, but you better have a balance.

ONE THOUSAND DOLLARS

IN THE WORDS of the great prophet Lil' Jon... OKAY! You've saved enough money to start investing (side note, I'd rather use the words *investing*, *investor*, and *investment* than *trading* because I feel like the action we take is trading, but the mentality has to be one of an investor. That's Wall Street-Smarts. So, I will use them both randomly). The amount you start with isn't important, but, of course, the more you have, the more you make. It really is a number's game; It's always about the numbers my friends. Trading with a small account takes so much more discipline than trading with a large one. The late, great trader prophet J. Livermore was quoted to say, "It is literally true that millions come easier to a trader after he knows how to trade than hundreds did in the days of his ignorance."

So, when we start with a small account with minimal capital, we have to think of ourselves being bigger one day, but now we're just a student of the game. To be fair, even if you start with a large account ($300K or so), I'd like you to understand that you are new in the game also. You just have more money to start with than the rest of us, but you have no experience, and you should act that way. Remember, you know nothing! #Humility

Speaking of Homies, Mr. Jim Cramer, (from the TV show "Mad Money") always tells his audience if you're getting started with that kind of cash, three hundred thousand, you should put the first ten thousand in an index fund $SPX $SPY (Vanguard funds) $VFINX or ETF's then start shopping and picking out investments that you can understand. So, homie is correct in his suggestion but that's if you're starting out with grands.

. . .

Most of us, ninety-nine percent of America, who only have Wall Street-Smarts are not starting out with 300k or even 10k. Most of us have to start right where we're at. That could mean five hundred or a thousand dollars for us. We *can't* just throw ten grand into an index fund or ETF's, yet. So, my encouragement to you is don't let any amount keep you out the game the Wall Street Game. #YouHeard

We're all quite ignorant (as in, not knowing) as to what the market has to offer us at the beginning. We know it's money, but the strategies still have to be executed on and experienced by you. We're also ignorant on what it can take from us in the beginning, so walk softly. Don't run, don't be in a rush to go broke or do something stupid. Another way of putting it is: feel free to get on the dance floor and dance, but dance close to the exits.

I'm suggesting for us to remain humble. Humble thyself—no one else can do it for you...but the market can.

I started with just $700 and, in less than seven months, grew the account to well over $13,000 including "contributions." Ever since that day, years later, I haven't had any less than that amount on any given day. Ask yourself, who do you know right now who keeps that kind of cash handy at all times... legally? If this book gets into the hands of those I know it can help, I already know the answer to that question, and so do you. Next time you ask yourself that question, let it be you with the cash. And that's my point; you don't have to be a millionaire or billionaire to be prosperous in the stock market.

You just have to have a way to prosper (hint: this Wall Street-Smarts series is a way). The stock market is one of the last institutions in America where you can actually get wealthy legally. I want to add that if you happen to be someone who does know quite a few people with thousands of dollars liquid at all times, then I'd like you to confirm with them what I have been writing about in this book. Ask any of them if they're invested into the stock market... I'll wait.

Try asking yourself another question (I keep asking you to do this because you will be surprised how many answers are already within you): if you were already a millionaire or a billionaire, where do you think you could legally park all that cash? Yep, the stock market and various other investment tools. Primarily, though, if you want to turn money into more money, the stock market is where that happens.

Now, when I talk about the liquid cash I have, I'm not gloating. I'm floating; that way no one knows I've passed them by. I will not be bragging about all the traveling I can do, the cars I own or the house I live in, nor will I be sporting around on Instagram the fine women sitting on my Lambo (mostly because I don't own a Lambo). Some of these other fools that do that stuff are a lot like those rap videos where the new rappers borrow the cars from a dealership to lean on. Then, later, when it's all a wrap, the brotha walks the streets and gets pushed up on for the Lambo money he doesn't have. (If I just called you a fool inadvertently, you probably still have time to change; we all do. Don't put your business on

FRONT St.) Mum's the word on the real streets, but on Wall Street and especially the social media platforms—Stocktwits, Reddit, Twitter—many will gloat, tote, and toot. As an old saying goes, if you don't toot your own horn every once in a while, you may never hear any music. I'm guessing many of these hot shots subscribe to this saying. So, I will only use real examples of personal finance when I'm sure it will benefit you, the thousandaire.

So, again, the amount of money you start with isn't important. What is important will be the amount you end up with. A well-known actor friend of mine started with just $500, and now he's a thousandaire in just a year. The dude was a millionaire in his day; he made the money as an actor, but the other smart people who were handling his finances broke him. #TrueStory

He has saved money and incurred profits by reinvesting dividends and compounding interest (look those terms up, dividends and compound interest especially, and learn how compound interest works;

it's amazing), and now he has more than $400 times a lot = a *lot*. Furthermore, he's able to grow his account on his own and use it for anything he wants. He travels the world a lot with his girlfriend.

Those of you with more than $1,000, good for you; I know you will get much out of this. But those of you who are starting with less than a thousand, keep your head up and be vigilant in your learning. You'll earn much more than that, and remember, before reading this book you probably didn't even have $400. Now that you do, I take my hat off to you and wish you all the best in becoming all you can be. #ArmedForces

Another suggestion I'd like to add is that early in the game, I didn't think of my account in the form of dollars; instead, I thought of every number in the account as points. I still do. I made it a habit of mines. So, I either made a lot of points today or I lost some for now but not forever. It helped me detach from the thought that I was losing or making money, because they were only points. Losing points hurt less than losing money. #RealTalk

> Try it. I think you'll find it useful.

Now, if any of you have any managerial or supervisory experience, you will find those skills very useful in managing a brokerage account. I was fortunate to have developed those skills first in the real streets and the black market and then professionally, with legitimate corporations such as Denny's, Grodins (retail store), and AM/PM convenience stores. Management skills will be highly useful when buying and selling equities. When you become a shareholder of a corporation, you have just bought a piece of that corporation; you own it. You can keep it forever or buy and sell at will. So, picking the corporations and the stocks you would like to invest into is all up to you; many other so-called stock pickers will tell you this is not as easy as it sounds. They all say this, over and over: "this is not easy as it sounds." Yes, it is. Straight out, they're lying again.

The financial shows do nothing but scare shareholders out of their shares, causing them to sell, sell, sell. Peter Lynch says to sell anything the TV financial analysts start promoting. Believe this, salesmen never stop selling and they always want to sell you the highest priced items. Picking stocks is easy, there's just quite a bit of due diligence you want to do before actually *buying* a stock of a corporation you may like. You want to give your pick the same attention you gave buying your home or car, that's all.

. . .

I will take you back to one of the most elementary examples I can think of. Imagine this: you're back in the middle school play yard, and you have to pick teams to play dodgeball. Now, you don't know every student or their abilities personally, but you might have heard about so and so being good at the game, and then you confirmed what you heard before picking them on your team.

Some of them you do know, and you know how good or bad they are at dodgeball. Then there are the losers you may have heard about, but you believe they are better than what people say. You look around at the selection; everyone knows that Jimmy is slow but can you use him, maybe he's a good blocker or something. Then you don't want to be an asshole and not pick any of the girls that want to play, so you pick the most athletic looking one, Sandy, not knowing if she can bring it or not. Now the whistle has blown and the game has started, and almost immediately at that unique moment, you realize you knew nothing about these players. You had no idea that Jimmy and Sandy were going to be your go-to players while the ones you at first thought were going to do well haven't, so now you have to bench them. And sometimes you find out that one of your picks is a "scaredy cat" and has to quit or get out the game. I just replicated a day of managing trades to you; you get it, right?

This is why adapting to the markets is a skill. It's fun, though, just like dodgeball, if you like to win like I do. There will be as many reasons to buy a stock as there are to sell it or not buy it at all. Pimps pick hoes the same way and manage them accordingly to profitability (a.k.a. ROI, Return On Investment); at the end of the evening, if she is lagging, he may cut her from the roster, and you may have to cut your stock the same way. (It's weird to me how I've been able to relate the observations of that darker world to this one on Wall St.—it can get dark on Wall St., too #Madoff—and in the government— the both of which I am sure are the biggest pimps of our time.) Side note: Did I fail to mention that the showrunner of the TV show "The Shield," said I was the best actor that played a pimp on that series? #5thSeason #Postpartum

. . .

Hiring managers and CEO's of businesses select employees in similar fashion, through a process using applications and interviews. You should be as diligent about selecting the stocks/equities in your portfolio. Develop the attitude of a business owner, because now you own a piece of a business/corporation, and the stocks will be working for you. They do well, you do well (usually). So, select a "team," a "block," a single first-round pick. Pick stocks that will work for you and make you profitable.

Peter Lynch is the dude I like to turn new investors onto to learn all about investing, trading, and especially how a thousandaire should go about picking their stocks. He's managed billions of dollars for Fidelity and has you covered when it comes to the technical indicators and the mathematics. (I like Fidelity for the small investor because they treat you big. Disclosure: they didn't pay me to say that.) Furthermore, Peter has a way of explaining the importance of risk management in very simple terms. Not in Wall Street-Smarts terms but in his terms. Peter's book subscribes to what the guru prophet Warren Buffett would say to someone looking to get into the stock market: "buy what you know." Don't buy corps (corporations) you know nothing about, especially in the beginning. Later on, when you've stacked some "cheddar," maybe then take the time to learn about something new to invest in. For now, "KISS" (Keep It Simple Strategy).

Peter's book is entitled *One Up On Wall Street*; google it, study it, and apply it.

So how should you start trading your undercapitalized account? With your objectives in place and loaded with an understanding that there's always a greater fool than you. We start with risk allocation; how much of the thousand should you risk?

Now, again, you're the boss of you, and you will have to determine your risk threshold. For learning purposes, though, let's talk some hypotheticals. Thresholds are usually discovered after one enters a trade. Like with the dodgeball game, you never know at first which players will bring it. Your stocks start moving up and down, and you'll need to be ready to take that money, let it ride, or only take a piece of the profits. All of these moves will be available to you once the exchange "bell" rings. But I'll do my best to describe what I mean by your risk threshold in the next book entitled *Turning Losers into Winners*. Together, along with one of the greatest American institutions still left in this country on our side, we can put an end to this crisis. #StayPaid

I won't leave you hanging. If you're loving what you're getting, and I have grabbed your attention and possibly adjusted your perception of these stock markets then you will be ready for more in *Turning Losers into Winners*. There we will discuss more about risk management, trade entry, and which account a thousandaire should get and you know how they say it, and much, much more!

In conclusion, I hope you found this information helpful. I'm not even rich yet, and when I say that I mean rich azz fu**! I do have fu** you money though. I feel rich most of the time. I figure in my own way, I am. I hope you play it cool. Keep your head in the Wall St. Game, and by all means, don't tell your friends, especially when you start making money. Wait 'til you made so much that they can't take it. Then tell 'em what you've been up to. Otherwise, just say all is well with your living when asked. #WallStreetSmarts

See ya in the next book.

THOUGHTS TO LIVE BY

1. There's always someone who is more foolish than you in the markets and you can rely on that fool to help you create your margin of safety.
2. No one runs you but you in these markets, and no one's going to shoot you if you get a trade wrong.
3. Skip that daily 3 lottery ticket and put that money into your free trading account and make you some real money.
4. Nobody knows everything. Most of us know nothing!
5. Don't worry about being like "Mike". Be you.

6. Once you know what you want, someone can't easily throw you off your game.
7. A greater fool, though, that's something you can count on.
8. Have no intentions of beating the markets ever.
9. I won't suggest to anyone that they should be in the market, but *everyone should be in the market*.
10. Buy low sell high, my friends, and don't let anyone tell you otherwise. IT STILL WORKS! IT'S AN UNDEFEATED METHOD!

SPENCER'S SOURCES

WEBSITES

- StockCharts
- Investors Hub
- TradingView
- Seeking Alpha
- Market Watch
- Small Cap Power
- FinViz (stock screener)
- Guru Focus
- The Fly
- Tiingo
- Earnings Cast Calls

SOCIAL MEDIA

StockTwits
FinTwit (Twitter)
Instagram
Reddit
Linkedin
Facebook

BOOKS

- Stock Trader's Almanac by Jeffrey A. Hirsch
- A Complete Guide to Volume Price Analysis by Anna Coulling
- Way of the Turtle by Curtis M. Faith
- Market Cycles by Howard Marks
- 100 Best Stocks to Buy in "(current year)" by Peter Sander and Scott Bobo
- Winning the Mental Game on Wall Street by John Magee
- What Works on Wall Street by Jim O'Shaughnessy
- Market Mind Games by Denise Shull
- Big Mistakes by Michael Batnick
- The New Market Wizards by Jack D. Schwager

- Your Money Your Brain by Jason Zweig
- The Little Book that Still Beats the Market by Joel Greenblatt
- An extra author for the list who writes really easy to understand stock market books is Matthew R. Kratter. Check him out on Amazon.

THOUSANDAIRE MOVEMENT

Thank you for purchasing this book and investing your time in reading it. It really means a lot to me. If you've enjoyed Wall Street Smarts, go ahead and join the Thousandaire Movement for updates, announcements and giveaways.

It's completely free to sign up and you will never be spammed by me. You can opt out easily at any time.

Go to www.wallstsmarts.com and join Thousandaire Movement by subscribing.

PLEASE LEAVE A REVIEW!

If you have enjoyed getting up on the game, I would be ever so grateful if you could spread the word.

With being a new author, reviews help me gain visibility and they can bring my books to the attention of other potential thousandaires who wish to improve their financial situations.

Leaving a review on Amazon helps others find this book more easily. Thank you in advance. #PayItForward

MORE BOOKS FROM YUL SPENCER

Turning Losers Into Winners In The Stock Market

Wall Street Game: Game Recognize Game

K.I.S.S. Keep It Simple Stock Market

For More Information
www.wallstsmarts.com

 facebook.com/WallStreetSmarts
 twitter.com/thewallstgame
 instagram.com/wallstsmarts

ABOUT THE AUTHOR

ABOUT THE AUTHOR

European born actor, **YUL SPENCER,** is a multi-talented performer whose career encompasses television, film, animation, theater, and standup comedy. As a comic, he went by the name of Spencer, toured nationally and has appeared on HBO, Comedy Central and eight seasons on BET's Comic-View. He has acted in hit TV shows like *The Shield and* Malcolm & Eddie, numerous films including *Two Can Play That Game* with Vivica A. Fox and various national commercials.

Yul was inspired for several reasons to write a series of books on the stock market, because many of his colleagues at his age had no "real" money. He was among comedians and actors living a high life because of who they are in the Hollywood industry, but none of them, including himself, had liquid cash or money they had saved. He thought what good is it to be a star at anything and not have access to a minimum of thousands of fu** you dollars.

After contemplating this lifestyle, he wanted to take back control of his finances. Yul wanted to determine how and when money came to him. So, he studied the market for the last ten years and read tons of books and wondered why more regular everyday people aren't investing. Well, what he found out, is that many of the trading books, make things way too complicated and confusing. They're discouraging to the average American. He wanted to write a series of books that offered more encouragement and simplified the way of profiting on the stock market. He felt, if he can do this, anyone can. Though, Yul was born in Europe, he was raised in Oakland, CA. Having been raised in Oakland, Yul has a lot of Street-Smarts, and he has applied his Street-Smarts and Comedy to the Stock Market, because the Stock Market has never been this funny.

These books were written "In response to America's $400.00 Financial crisis." Everyone should have at the very least $400.00 available to them at all times. At his core, Yul believes Americans can put an end to "brokeness" that plagues most citizens. He feels it's time for us all to come up and not let an unexpected $400.00 bill throw us into disarray.

FULL DISCLAIMER

While the author has used his best efforts in preparing this book, he makes no representations or warranties with respect to the accuracy or completeness of the contents of this book and specifically disclaims any implied warranties or merchantability or fitness for a particular purpose. The advice and strategies contained herein may not be suitable for your situation.

You should consult with a legal, financial, tax professional where appropriate. Neither the publisher nor the author shall be liable for any loss of profit or any other commercial damages, including but not limited to special, incidental, consequential, or other damages.

FULL DISCLAIMER

This book is for educational, informational and entertainment purposes only. The views expressed are those of the author alone and should not be taken as expert instruction or commands. The reader is responsible for his or her own actions.

Adherence to all applicable laws and regulations, including international, federal, state, and local laws, is the sole responsibility of the purchaser or reader.

Neither the author nor the publisher assumes any responsibility or liability whatsoever on the behalf of the purchaser or reader of these materials.

Any perceived slight of any individual or organization is purely unintentional.

Past performance is not necessarily indicative of future performance.

Forex, futures, stock and options trading is not appropriate for everyone.

There is a substantial risk of loss associated with trading these markets. Losses can and will occur.

No system or methodology has ever been developed that can guarantee profits of ensure freedom from losses. Nor will it likely ever be.

No representation or implication is being made that using the methodologies or systems or the information contained within this book will generated profits or ensure freedom from losses.

The information contained in this book is for educational, informational and entertainment purposes only and should NOT be taken as investment advice. Examples presented here are not solicitations to buy or sell. The author, publisher, and all affiliates assume no responsibility for your trading results.

THERE IS HIGH RISK IN TRADING!

Copyright © 2020 by IAM Enterprises

All rights reserved.

No part of this book may be reproduced in any form or by any electronic or mechanical means, including information storage and retrieval systems, without written permission from the author, except for the use of brief quotations in a book review.

First Printing, 2020

IAM Enterprises
P. O. Box 17274
Encino, CA 91416

www.wallstsmarts.com

www.ingramcontent.com/pod-product-compliance
Lightning Source LLC
Chambersburg PA
CBHW070245220526
45465CB00004B/1527